GoPro Hero 13 User Guide

A Practical Manual for Photographers of All Levels to Master the GoPro Hero 13 Camera

Katherine K. Tucker

Copyright

Copyright @2024 (**Patrick Putnam**) All rights reserved. No part of this publication may be reproduced, distributed, or transmitted in any form or by any means, including photocopying, recording, or other electronic or mechanical methods, without the prior written permission of the author, except in the case of brief quotations embodied in critical reviews and certain other noncommercial uses permitted by copyright law.

This book is a work of the author and has been written with the intention to educate and inspire. The views expressed herein are those of the author and do not necessarily reflect the views of the publisher.

Table of content

Chapter 1..5
    Understanding Your Hero 13. GoPro..................5

Chapter 2..9
    Secrets of Capturing Motion in Action Photography... 9

Chapter 3..16
    Creating Smooth, Vivid Video in High-Action Scenarios... 16

Chapter 4..23
    Using Action Shots to Tell Stories.................... 23

Chapter 5..28
    Mastering Light in Dynamic Environments......28
    Recognizing various light sources..................... 29
    Understanding Exposure Configurations.......... 30
    Methods for Changing the Lighting..................31
    Innovative use of shadows................................ 33
    Practical Use..36

Chapter 6..38
    Editing for Impact... 38
    Selecting the Best Editing Software to Get Started... 39
    Basic Action Shot Editing Techniques..............40

Sophisticated editing methods for impactful effects.. 42
Using editing to create a story........................... 43
Example from the Real World........................... 46

Chapter 7.. 48
Advanced Tips for Different Action Environments.. 48
Urban Environments.. 48
Natural Settings.. 50
Adjusting to various weather situations............ 54
Examples from the Real World:........................ 56

Chapter 8.. 58
Gear and Accessories for Extreme Action Photography.. 58
Important GoPro add-ons for adventurous photographers.. 59
Professional Suggestions for Particular Action Situations... 62

Conclusion... 66
Becoming a GoPro Action Storyteller.............. 66

Chapter 1

Understanding Your Hero 13. GoPro

The GoPro Hero 13 is a strong tool that will improve your action photography and cinematography; it's more than simply a camera. This chapter will walk you through the capabilities of its hardware and software, assist you in adjusting settings for best results, and offer crucial pointers for properly configuring your camera. Gaining an understanding of your GoPro Hero 13 will enable you to realize its full potential and produce breathtaking images in any setting. The GoPro Hero 13's hardware is remarkable, with a sturdy construction that can resist weather conditions. Its 23MP sensor produces high-resolution images, and its 5.3K video recording at 60 frames per second guarantees that even the most dramatic moments are captured with breathtaking clarity. You may easily photograph large scenes thanks to the camera's lens's wide field of view. Even in the most chaotic situations, the integrated HyperSmooth stabilization technology elevates your footage by reducing shaking and vibrations to provide results that seem professional.

In terms of software, the Hero 13 has an intuitive interface that makes adjusting its settings simple. Because of the sensitive touchscreen, you can review your film or make quick adjustments to the settings. The Hero 13's sophisticated HDR capabilities are one of its best qualities; they increase the dynamic range of your photos and make them vivid and detailed even in difficult lighting situations. A variety of shooting modes are also available on the camera, including TimeWarp, which records time-lapse videos while you move, and SuperPhoto, which automatically enhances your photos with HDR and noise reduction. Adjusting your settings according to the kind of action shots you wish to take is essential if you want to fully utilize the GoPro Hero 13's capabilities. To guarantee fluid playback during fast-paced activities like mountain biking or skiing, set your video resolution to 4K at 120 frames per second. To capture more of the scene, set the field of view to "Wide." For stabilized video, turn on HyperSmooth. If you're shooting in low light, don't forget to turn on the low-light mode. This will maximize the camera's capabilities and provide sharper pictures.

Setting up the camera is just as crucial to getting excellent results. For steady shots, your GoPro must be mounted correctly. For action sports, think about utilizing a chest mount, which frees up your hands and offers a first-person viewpoint. A helmet mount can provide a higher perspective of the action during outdoor excursions. Make sure your camera is always firmly attached to avoid any unintentional drops. Another crucial component of camera setup is stabilization. Although the Hero 13's HyperSmooth technology is revolutionary, you can improve stability even more by maintaining steady, fluid motions. Try to predict your subject's movements while filming and modify your position accordingly. For instance, to keep a continuous frame when photographing a skateboarder, move in time with their direction.

Finally, before you set out on your excursion, make sure to verify your storage capacity and battery life. If you use a high-capacity microSD card and carry an extra battery, you won't miss a second of action because high-resolution videos consume more space and power. Now that you have a firm grasp of your GoPro Hero 13's capabilities and know how to set it up, you can begin taking breathtaking action photos that will convey your story in ways you never thought possible.

Chapter 2

Secrets of Capturing Motion in Action Photography

Every photographer faces the exciting task of capturing motion, which is similar to freezing time, particularly in dynamic scenes.

Henri Cartier-Bresson, the renowned photographer famously remarked, "Everything in this world has a decisive moment." This idea is especially relevant to action photography, where accuracy and timing are crucial. How well you can capture the intensity and thrill of the moment depends on your ability to frame dynamic pictures, whether you're shooting fast-paced sports, scuttling wildlife, or busy city scenes.

Knowing the surroundings is essential when framing dynamic photos in fast-moving situations. Each setting is distinct and has a varied set of possibilities and difficulties. For example, sports photography requires a strong sense of the game in addition to rapid reactions. Experience builds the ability to predict where the action will take place. Think about the instant a soccer player is about to take a penalty kick. Your camera should be positioned to capture the intensity of the electrifying atmosphere. It's all about positioning. Being in the correct place may make all the difference, whether you're at a street festival or watching a football game. Recognize the most advantageous viewpoints. You can have a better perspective of the action in sports by standing higher or having sideline access. Patience may be needed when taking wildlife photos, as you may need to wait in blindness or use a longer lens to maintain your distance while still catching fine details of the animal's activities.

The scene in street photography frequently develops in an unpredictable way. You'll need to learn to trust your gut when it comes to pressing the shutter. There is potential for breathtaking photos when people move across space in a dance. Seek out interactions, such as a couple laughing together, a toddler splashing through puddles, or a street entertainer enthralling an audience. You can record genuine, unscripted moments in these situations by blending in with the surroundings and making use of the GoPro Hero 13's discrete small size.

After positioning yourself, the next step is to become proficient in timing, focus, and angling—all of which are essential for action photos. Timing is divided into two parts: reaction and anticipation. Anticipation entails forecasting the occurrence of a momentous occasion. For instance, you want to be prepared to catch the cyclist at the top of their game while you're taking pictures of them approaching a turn. Conversely, reaction is about being ready for everything that might happen. More practice with the motion you're filming will improve this.

Your timing and attentiveness can be improved with practical activities. Practicing shooting at a busy park or local sporting event is one efficient way. Put your GoPro Hero 13 in burst mode so you may take multiple pictures every second. For subjects that move quickly, this setting is ideal since it improves your chances of catching the perfect moment.

Start by concentrating on just one thing, such as a dog chasing a ball or a friend skateboarding. Use your camera to follow their movements and change focus as necessary. This practice keeps your reflexes sharp while teaching you to follow the action. After that, go over your shots. Note which photos capture the event's spirit and which don't. Knowing your talents and places for development is made much easier with the help of this reflection.

Practice panning as well; it's a skill that can significantly improve your action photography. In order to convey a sensation of speed while maintaining subject focus, panning entails moving your camera in time with a moving subject. Start with anything that moves slowly, such as a car driving down a street. As the car gets closer, start following it with your camera, keeping your eye on it while you press the shutter. Lower the shutter speed. The outcome is a clear foreground with a blurred background that successfully captures motion.

Because of the GoPro Hero 13's adaptability, you may improve your images by using its many settings. Even in difficult lighting conditions, the SuperPhoto function automatically applies HDR processing to your photos, bringing out details and guaranteeing that highlights and shadows are precisely balanced. In fast-paced settings where lighting can change rapidly, such as during a soccer match where players rush across the field from blinding sun to deep shadow, this is very helpful. For optimal SuperPhoto performance, familiarize yourself with your lighting. SuperPhoto can enhance your photos by highlighting rich colors and textures that would otherwise be missed, such as during sunrise or sunset, when the light is low but dramatic. It's revolutionary for taking striking action photos. For high-motion photos, GoPro's HDR settings are just as important. HDR can assist you in capturing the entire spectrum of tones when there are sharp contrasts between light and shadow. Without HDR, you risk losing details in the dark shadows and bright highlights when photographing a mountain cyclist racing through a forest that is dappled by the sun. When HDR is turned on, the camera balances the light and produces a gorgeously detailed picture by combining several exposures into a single shot.

To give your action photography more dimension, you can also think about creatively framing your photos. Include aspects of the surroundings that add to the tale you're conveying, rather than only concentrating on the main topic. For instance, if you're taking a picture of a skateboarder, think about capturing the eager crowd in the background or the graffiti on the surrounding wall. These components can add context and enhance the visual appeal of your photos.

Try a variety of viewpoints and perspectives. A photo of a runner can be made more dramatic by lowering your camera to the ground, which gives them a stronger appearance against the track's background. As an alternative, photographing a scene from above might offer a distinctive perspective that distinguishes your work. Because of its small size, the GoPro Hero 13 may be mounted in unusual locations, such as on a skateboard's side, on a pet, or even on a drone for amazing aerial photography.

Keep in mind that practice makes perfect. Go out and try out various methods and environments. To gain feedback on your work, go to local events or join a photographic group. Push yourself to venture beyond your comfort zone and attempt new things. You'll discover that every action photography session offers fresh chances for improvement as you continue to refine your craft. Don't be scared to make mistakes along the way; instead, embrace the learning process. Every picture you snap is an opportunity to record a moment in time that might not come along again.

In the end, it takes ingenuity, experience, and observation to become an expert at framing dynamic pictures in fast-paced environments. With the correct methods and the GoPro Hero 13's strong features at your disposal, you'll have no trouble taking breathtaking pictures that capture the spirit and thrill of any journey. The possibilities are infinite as you embark on your adventure in the realm of action photography. So prepare yourself, go out, and express your talent!

Chapter 3

Creating Smooth, Vivid Video in High-Action Scenarios

It can seem impossible to make videos that capture the spirit of activity, particularly when everything around you is changing all the time. However, by utilizing the GoPro Hero 13's 4K and 5K video capabilities, you can elevate your footage from average to exceptional, giving adventure sports fans and travel content producers the breathtaking quality they desire.

The Hero 13 is more than just another action camera; it's a technological powerhouse that will enhance your narrative with striking images. Using its 4K and 5K capabilities, you'll learn how to turn every frame into a motion picture. Let's first discuss how these resolutions will affect your film before getting into the details. With four times the resolution of 1080p HD, 4K video produces remarkably detailed and clear images. This is particularly crucial when capturing fast-paced sports where attention to detail is essential, like surfing or mountain biking. Moments that tell a story, like the sunshine glinting off the waves or the dirt kicking up from the tires, are what you want to capture. You can attain an even more amazing degree of clarity and detail by making use of the Hero 13's 5K capability. More post-production freedom is made possible by this higher resolution, which lets you crop or zoom in on your images without compromising quality. Imagine keeping the crisp clarity that makes your movie stand out while simultaneously shooting a broad view of a snow-capped mountain range and then focusing in on a skier as they make their way down the slope.

Knowing your surroundings and lighting conditions is crucial to maximizing these talents. For example, shooting during the golden hour, which is just after dawn or before sunset, gives your photos that warm, diffused light that brings out the colors and depth. The Hero 13's sophisticated HDR (High Dynamic Range) features come into action in direct sunlight, enabling you to avoid blown-out highlights and capture a wider variety of tones.

It's simple to set up your GoPro, but remember that composition and framing are crucial. When filming action, aim to maintain your subject's focus while letting the background tell the story. By providing context, this method gives the audience the impression that they are a part of the journey. If you're recording a rock climber, for example, you may get a dynamic shot that highlights the climber and the stunning cliff face they're scaling by putting the camera slightly below and to the side.

Your shot consistency is as important as your footage quality. GoPro's HyperSmooth technology excels in this situation. Picture yourself racing down a rough track on a mountain bike, where roots and pebbles could jostle your camera. The purpose of HyperSmooth is to remove unsteady footage, which can detract from otherwise flawless shots. It produces smooth, high-quality video by analyzing and compensating for your camera's movements using sophisticated algorithms.

With HyperSmooth 5.0, stability is elevated to a new level. It adjusts for both the subject's and the camera's movements. This implies that you may record the action without worrying about shaky footage, even in the most chaotic situations—like an exhilarating white-water rafting excursion. However, knowing the many settings available is necessary to get the best outcomes.

You can choose between two modes when HyperSmooth is activated: "On" mode delivers excellent stabilization in most situations, while "Boost" setting offers even more aggressive stabilization, making it ideal for extreme sports like motocross or skydiving. Particularly in settings with lots of action, the distinction between the two can be quite noticeable. You can better grasp how these settings impact your final result by experimenting with them in various contexts.

Another crucial element of producing fluid and vibrant video is choosing the right frame rate. You can select from a range of frame rates with the GoPro Hero 13 based on your shooting requirements. 30 frames per second (fps) is typically enough for typical action video. However, increasing the frame rate to 60 frames per second can improve the quality of your footage if you're recording fast-paced sports or want to convey a sense of urgency.

Use a slower frame rate for those scenes where you want to create a dramatic impression. You can record slow-motion footage that can transform an average action scene into an amazing visual experience by shooting at 120 frames per second or even 240 frames per second. Imagine a skateboarder soaring through the air; you can highlight their talent and grace of movement by slowing down the video at greater frame rates.

Furthermore, the Hero 13 strikes a fantastic balance between rapid action and high quality thanks to its 5K 60 fps shooting capability. Because of its adaptability, you can combine various frame rates and resolutions in your edits to produce an engaging narrative flow. To improve the overall storytelling, it can be as simple as alternating between conventional speed for the majority of your film and slow motion for some moments. Think about doing hands-on activities that concentrate on stabilizing your photos and playing with frame rates to hone your skills. Spend a day filming your buddies doing anything they want, like riding their bikes, skateboarding, or just playing in the park. To determine which HyperSmooth setting is most effective in each situation, experiment with the various settings. Pay attention to how the stabilization affects your video's feel and how you might make the most of it.

Try recording the same action under various settings to see how frame rates change. Take a brief video of someone jumping off a swing at 30 frames per second and then again at 120 frames per second, for instance. Examine the video and note how the increased frame rate alters how movement is perceived. This activity will teach you how to communicate various emotions in your movies in addition to helping you comprehend the technical aspects of frame rates. Consider how you may improve your videos in post-production as you get more experience. You may change your clips' colors, contrast, and even pace with the aid of editing tools. With the help of GoPro's easy-to-use editing app, which seamlessly connects to your camera, you can rapidly gather your film, make the required edits, and share it with the world.

There are countless opportunities and a lot of excitement in the field of action photography and filming. You have everything you need to produce breathtaking videos that perfectly capture the excitement of the moment with the GoPro Hero 13. Your journey is just getting started, whether you're biking down a route, climbing a mountain, or discovering a new city. You may turn your footage from average to exceptional by learning how to use its 4K and 5K capabilities, comprehending HyperSmooth technology, and choosing the appropriate frame rates. Then, you can share your footage with other adventure sports lovers and travel content creators. So get your GoPro, go outside, and start exploring!

Chapter 4

Using Action Shots to Tell Stories

The goal of action photography is to tell a story that connects with your audience, not only to capture a moment in time. Using action photos to tell captivating stories makes your work stand out in this digital age where everyone has access to a camera. Even in impromptu situations, the GoPro Hero 13 gives you the means to turn everyday experiences into gripping narratives.

Think like a filmmaker when you're planning a sequence. A successful story has a beginning, middle, and end and develops over time. Even in situations that move quickly, you can take a sequence of pictures that together make a story. Imagine the scene first. What do you want to portray? Your story might center on a skater's quest to master a trick if you're at a skatepark. Your sequence may start with the skater getting ready, then move in, perform the trick, and end with a hilarious wipeout or a successful landing.

Being adaptable is essential in impromptu circumstances. Having a mental storyboard might help you navigate situations where you are unable to forecast exactly what will happen next. If you're at a music festival, for instance, make plans to record the minutes before an artist makes their big revelation. Record the enthusiastic mood, the artist's preparations, and the emotions of the audience. This method immerses viewers in the event while simultaneously capturing the activity.

Using point-of-view (POV) viewpoints can give your narrative a more intimate feel. You can establish a close relationship with your viewers by holding the camera at eye level or securing it to your subject, whether they are a pet, a bicycle, or a snowboarder. They get a close look at the thrills and spills, feeling as though they are a part of the action. Because of its small size and adaptability, the GoPro Hero 13 can be mounted in a variety of locations and offers distinctive viewpoints that conventional cameras just cannot match.

Think about the impact that various perspectives can have on the narrative. By making the person seem larger than life, a low-angle image can communicate strength and authority. A high-angle photography, on the other hand, can convey vulnerability. Try different angles: raise the camera to obtain a more expansive view of the action, or get down low for a rough, ground-level shot. For extra vitality, you might even mix different angles in your sequence, alternating between broader frames and point-of-view shots to create context.

Another essential skill for action photographers is the ability to shoot while moving. Your technique and camera settings are the keys to consistently good film. Make every effort to stabilize your movements when you're photographing dynamic moments. When jogging or moving, use your body as a stabilizer by keeping your arms close to your body and bending your knees slightly. By using this method, you may reduce jolts and rattles and produce smoother video. This is where the HyperSmooth feature of the GoPro Hero 13 is useful. This cutting-edge stabilizing mechanism smoothes out any bumps you may experience when moving. Be sure to become acquainted with the various HyperSmooth settings. "Boost" setting can greatly improve stabilization in fast-paced situations, giving your video a polished appearance.

For the purpose of storytelling, footage must be consistent. Take into account the following strategies to do this:

Keep the Frame Rate Consistent: Throughout the shot, keep your frame rate constant. This guarantees that your footage has a consistent appearance and feel, which facilitates seamless shot transitions. To ensure consistency, stick with your choice of 60 or 120 frames per second. Employ a Consistent White Balance: Particularly outside, lighting conditions can vary quickly. Maintaining color uniformity throughout your images and avoiding flickering can be achieved by using a preset white balance. Use the "Native" preset if you're shooting in mixed lighting, as it gives you more post-production options.

Establish a Consistent Editing Procedure: Following the capture of your footage, create a consistent editing procedure. To make your style cohesive, arrange your clips according to sequences and use comparable color grading and effects. This guarantees that your photos will merge together in the finished product even if they were taken at different frame speeds or in different lighting situations.

Narrative Hooks: Consider how to develop captivating narrative hooks when editing. Start with a captivating image, such as a close-up of a sportsman getting ready for a breathtaking scene that establishes the mood. Next, incorporate layers into your sequence so that each shot builds on the one before it, generating excitement and suspense. You can improve the narrative element of your action photos by concentrating on these strategies. Never forget that every frame matters. Creating an immersive experience that keeps your audience interested and involved in the story you're telling is your aim from the very beginning of planning to the very end of editing.

Chapter 5

Mastering Light in Dynamic Environments

One of the most important yet frequently disregarded aspects of photography is mastering light in dynamic settings, particularly when utilizing action cameras like the GoPro Hero 13. Knowing how to control and adjust to changing light conditions may greatly improve the quality of your photos and movies, whether you're photographing a mountain biker racing through a deep forest or a surfer riding the top of a wave at sunset. This chapter delves deeply into the subtleties of lighting, providing useful methods, real-world examples, and crucial advice to help you produce breathtaking effects in any situation.

The essence of photography is light, which may direct the viewer's eye and arouse feelings and mood. The difficulty in dynamic surroundings is that light can change quickly; dazzling reflections can be distracting, clouds can block the sun, or shadows can vary. Therefore, mastering light requires not just knowledge of its characteristics but also a sharp sense of awareness and flexibility.

Recognizing various light sources

Understanding the various sources of light is the first step toward mastering it. Weather, the season, and geographic location all have an impact on natural light, which can change significantly during the day. Shortly after sunrise and before sunset, the golden hour is praised for its gentle, warm light that makes people look beautiful. Colors are more intense, and shadows are longer during this period.

But what occurs when you're in an environment with intense sunlight or clouds? Overexposed whites or underexposed darks are frequently the result of harsh sunlight's ability to create dramatic highlights and shadows. Cloudy days, on the other hand, offer a gentle, diffused light that lessens shadows and makes it possible to expose your subjects more evenly. It's critical to quickly adjust to these shifts in dynamic circumstances, like action sports or travel situations. The GoPro Hero 13's settings allow you to adjust for different lighting conditions. For example, putting the camera in "Auto" mode can help it adjust the exposure automatically, and utilizing "Spot Meter" can guarantee that the subject is illuminated correctly even if the background is significantly darker or brighter.

Understanding Exposure Configurations

Understanding your camera's exposure settings aperture, shutter speed, and ISO is essential to becoming a true light expert. Every one of these components is essential to the way light affects your photos.

1. Aperture: This determines the amount of light that enters the camera. While a tighter aperture (higher f-stop number) decreases light and improves depth of field, bringing more of the picture into focus, a wider aperture (lower f-stop number) lets in more light, which is especially helpful in low light.

2. Shutter Speed: The duration of light exposure to the camera's sensor is determined by the shutter speed. A faster shutter speed is necessary to freeze the action in fast-moving scenarios, such as a skateboarder completing tricks. On the other hand, a slower shutter speed can produce a feeling of motion, which is helpful for expressing dynamism and speed.

3. ISO: It gauges how sensitive a camera is to light. In darker environments, a higher ISO can be useful, but it also adds noise to your photos. Maintaining image quality while attaining the right exposure requires balancing ISO, aperture, and shutter speed.

Utilize the GoPro Hero 13's sophisticated controls to modify exposure based on your surroundings. When filming a bike racing through a sun-dappled forest, for example, you might need to raise the ISO to capture the abrupt changes in light as the cyclist enters and exits shadows.

Methods for Changing the Lighting

You may efficiently master light in dynamic surroundings by using certain approaches. Here are a few strategies to think about:

• **Use Reflectors and Diffusers:** Without modifying camera settings, reflectors can re-bounce light onto your subject, bringing shadowy parts to life. For example, utilizing a reflector can help fill in the shadows on a snowboarder's face while you're filming them against a brilliant blue sky. Conversely, diffusers soften intense light. A diffuser between your subject and the sun might help provide more flattering light while you're shooting in direct sunshine.

• **RAW photography:** RAW photography gives you more post-processing options when dealing with challenging lighting circumstances. Compared to JPEGs, RAW files store more information, which makes it simpler to modify exposure, highlights, shadows, and white balance without sacrificing image quality. When you have a variety of lighting sources, like a sunset with artificial lights in the foreground, this is really helpful.

• **Manual White Balance:** When shooting in situations where the light is changing rapidly, the GoPro Hero 13's manual white balance settings can be extremely helpful. Set the white balance based on the particular lighting circumstances rather than depending on the camera's automatic adjustments. For instance, a custom white balance can help you keep your photos' colors consistent even if you're shooting in a shady place with some sunshine.

Innovative use of shadows

You may use shadows to your advantage while making striking pictures. Consider how you may employ shadows to give your photos depth, drama, and interest rather than ignoring them. For example, capturing the runner's extended shadow on the pavement at sunrise might add to the image's feeling of motion and vitality.

When framing your photographs, take the light's direction into account as well. Strong contrasts and textures can be produced by side lighting, in which the light source is positioned to the side. Backlighting, on the other hand, can highlight features like hair or water droplets or provide lovely silhouettes when the light source is behind your subject.

Time and place

When it comes to light, timing is everything. The way light falls on your subject is affected by the sun's location, which varies throughout the day.

Investigate areas at various times to learn how light affects particular areas. For example, if you want to take pictures on a mountain bike trail, go there at the same time of day. Take note of any problematic regions, including strong highlights or deep shadows, as well as how the light interacts with the terrain.

The actual location can have a big impact on light in trip photography. For example, negotiating artificial lighting sources like neon signs and street lamps is frequently necessary when filming in an urban setting. These lights can produce dramatic contrasts with the waning natural light at sunset, opening up artistic possibilities. Place yourself such that your subject can be framed by the ambient light from buildings without overpowering the natural light.

Getting Used to Change

Adapting to change is one of the biggest obstacles to mastering light in dynamic surroundings. Rapid changes in the weather are possible; clouds may roll in, the sun may disappear behind a mountain, or the sky may abruptly turn cloudy. It's critical for photographers to be ready to adjust their settings.

To assist with this, think about utilizing the features on your GoPro Hero 13. With the help of the camera's live view, you can quickly make modifications by seeing the effects of changing settings in real time. You can swiftly raise the ISO or widen the aperture without losing the shot if you discover that your picture is underexposed because of an unexpected cloud cover.

Carry a portable light source as well, like an LED panel or even a torch for your smartphone. When photographing in areas with a lot of shadows or in low light, these can be used as fill light. Without dominating the prevailing light, a tiny LED can give just enough illumination to draw attention to your subject's face.

After-Processing Methods

Last but not least, mastering light extends beyond simply taking pictures; post-processing is an effective technique that may greatly improve your images. You can adjust exposure, contrast, and color balance using programs like Adobe Lightroom or Photoshop to fix any irregularities brought on by changing lighting.

Keep your eye on the histogram, which shows the tonal values in your picture visually. A balanced histogram that avoids extending too far into the highlights or shadows is what you want. To recover details, try lowering exposure or removing highlights if you think the photo is too bright.

Gradient filters are another crucial post processing method. In order to prevent either being blown out or lost in shadow, these filters can assist in balancing exposure between brilliant skies and darker landscapes. More control over the finished image can be achieved by using a gradient filter in software that can replicate the effects of real filters used while shooting.

Practical Use

Let's examine a real-world situation to illustrate these ideas. Consider that you are photographing a friend at a nearby skate park while they are skateboarding. Deep shadows and vivid highlights are produced by the strong light from the high-altitude sun.

To find the ideal shooting angles and times, start by inspecting the area. You might discover that a captivating context is created by photographing the skateboarder and the bowl from the same viewpoint.

Flip through your GoPro Hero 13's settings while your pal skates. Use a faster shutter speed when they perform a trick so that you can freeze the action while still catching the dynamic surroundings. Try using tighter frames as well as broad shots to capture the spirit of the occasion.

Make real-time adjustments to your settings if the sun unexpectedly disappears behind a cloud. Maybe raise the ISO to make up for the abrupt decrease in light. If necessary, use reflectors to refract light into your friend's face. Examine your movie after shooting, then edit the best parts using post-processing techniques to bring out the details buried in shadows and improve the colors.

Chapter 6

Editing for Impact

Bringing Your Action Shots to Life

In photography, editing is where the real magic happens, particularly in action photos. Using the GoPro Hero 13 to record dynamic moments is only the first step; the true art is in how you edit such moments to improve them. The tools, methods, and imaginative approaches for editing your action shots to produce gripping stories that captivate audiences and give your photos life are covered in detail in this chapter.

Editing's Significance in Action Photography

There are several uses for editing in action photography. It may improve aesthetic appeal, fix technical issues, and—above all—tell a story. Even if an action shot that hasn't been edited could catch an exciting moment, it frequently lacks the emotional impact that careful editing can provide. Editing helps you hone your vision, whether you're cropping for a better composition, altering exposure levels, or applying color grading to set the mood.

In the current digital era, when people are consuming pictures at a quick pace, captivating images can significantly impact audience engagement. Whether it's the calm beauty of a surfer riding a wave at dawn or the exhilaration of a skateboarder soaring through the air, a well-edited action image may arouse feelings in addition to drawing attention.

Selecting the Best Editing Software to Get Started

Choosing the appropriate program is the first step in editing your action shots. Numerous choices are available, each with unique characteristics to meet distinct editing requirements. Popular options consist of:

• **Adobe Lightroom:** Lightroom is well-known for its extensive features designed specifically for photographers, including tools for modifying color, contrast, and exposure. Its user-friendly interface makes it simple to apply comparable adjustments to several photos and is ideal for batch processing.

• **Adobe Photoshop:** Photoshop is the best option for more complex editing. Layer-based editing, fine-grained retouching, and complex transformations are all possible with it. Photoshop is the best option if you need to make significant edits or artistic composites for your action images.

• **GoPro Quik:** Made especially for GoPro users, Quik is a powerful tool for fast video editing. Action footage may benefit greatly from its ability to automatically edit clips to music and produce highlight reels.

• **Mobile Apps:** Snapseed and VSCO are two examples of mobile apps that offer convenient tools for color correction, cropping, and filter applications right from your smartphone for fast edits while on the road.

Basic Action Shot Editing Techniques

It's important to comprehend some basic editing techniques that can greatly improve your action shots before attempting more complex ones.

1. Cropping for Composition: Your original composition is frequently not flawless. Among the most important tools for improving frames is cropping. For a more interesting composition, crop your subject along the lines or intersections using the rule of thirds as a guide.

2. Modifying Exposure and Contrast: When shooting in dynamic settings, action photographs may suffer from overexposed highlights or underexposed shadows. Adjust the contrast to give your photos depth, make them stand out, and use the exposure slider to fix any inconsistencies.

3. Color Correction: Depending on the camera settings and lighting, action images may have different hues. To make colors seem realistic, use white balance changes. The brilliance of your photos can be significantly increased by adjusting the tint and temperature.

4. Sharpening and Noise Reduction: Noise can be a major problem with action photography, especially in low light. Grainy areas can be smoothed out while maintaining details by using noise reduction techniques. To improve the edges and highlight the clarity in your action images, sharpen them afterwards.

Sophisticated editing methods for impactful effects

After you've mastered the fundamentals, think about investigating more complex methods that can help you improve your action shots.

1. Producing a Cinematic Look: Color grading is an effective storytelling technique. You can arouse specific feelings by using a particular color scheme. Warm, golden hues, for instance, may generate feelings of nostalgia, whereas colder hues can promote serenity. To modify hues and saturation, use tools like color balance and curves.

2. Dynamic Cropping and Panning: Take into account dynamic cropping methods for action images that show movement. This entails cropping the frame's edges just enough to convey motion and urgency. When used with motion blur effects, this can portray enthusiasm and speed.

3. Including Textures and Overlays: Using textures can give your photos more depth. Without overpowering the main image, subtle overlays like grain or light leaks can add motion or convey a vintage vibe. Just make sure you keep things in proportion so the impact enhances rather than detracts from the image.

4. Making Use of Layers and Masks: Selective editing is made possible in Photoshop via layers and masks. To properly balance the lighting, for example, if your subject is well-lit but the background is not, you can make a mask that only makes exposure adjustments to the background.

Using editing to create a story

Editing involves more than just making technical changes; it also involves creating a story. The editing process has the power to bring out the narrative in each action shot. Here are some tips for using editing to produce an engaging story:

1. Sequence Editing: Take into account the arrangement of your action shots when creating video material. A skillfully written scene can increase tension while guiding the audience through a plot point. To keep the action moving and the audience interested, carefully consider your cuts and transitions.

2. Thematic Consistency: It's crucial to keep your style consistent when working on a video montage or a collection of pictures. This entails employing comparable color grading, cropping techniques, and effects to produce a unified story that seems deliberate and well-curated.

3. Emphasizing Emotions: Pay attention to situations that make you feel something. Choosing images that express emotion and enhancing them with editing can increase the impact of your work, whether that feeling is the calm of nature or the thrill of victory.

A realistic action shot editing process

Consider using the following useful workflow to expedite your editing process:

1. Import and Arrange: Open your editing program and import your action photos first. For better access, group them into collections or folders according to locations, events, or themes.

2. First Evaluation and Selection: Examine your photos and pick the best ones. Seek out pictures that, whether through action, expression, or arrangement, have the biggest effect.

3. Simple Edits: Begin with simple edits such as color correction, contrast, cropping, and exposure. Make an effort to raise the general caliber of the pictures you have chosen.

4. Advanced methods: Use advanced methods like color grading, layering, and texture addition after the fundamentals are finished. Try a variety of approaches until you discover one that improves your story.

5. Last Review and Export: To guarantee consistency and quality, conduct a last review once you are happy with your adjustments. After that, export your photos in the format that best suits your needs, be it video, prints, or social media.

Example from the Real World

Editing an Action Shot

Imagine capturing an exhilarating moment of a mountain cyclist negotiating a precipitous drop. It was difficult to see because of the stark contrasts caused by the bright sunshine filtered through the trees.

When you import the picture into your editing program, you see that the tree shadows are excessively dark and the biker's helmet highlights are blown out. To bring out more detail in the woods, adjust the exposure to reduce highlights and increase shadows.

The rider is then positioned slightly off-center to produce a more dramatic composition by cropping the picture to follow the rule of thirds. The image's overall ambiance is then improved by experimenting with color grading and choosing a slightly colder tone to portray the clear mountain air.

In order to give the picture a rugged feel and go with the bicycle theme, you add a little texture overlay at the end. You export the picture after making a few little changes, eager to highlight the ride's excitement.

Chapter 7

Advanced Tips for Different Action Environments

Knowing your surroundings is just as important for taking action photos as knowing your camera's settings. From busy metropolitan streets to serene natural settings, every environment offers different opportunities and difficulties. In order to help you adapt your GoPro Hero 13 abilities to varied situations and guarantee that you obtain the finest shots possible, regardless of where your travels take you, this chapter delves into advanced advice designed for a variety of action environments.

Urban Environments

Embracing the City's Vitality

Urban environments are ideal for action photography because they are frequently lively and dynamic. But there are drawbacks to the bustle of a metropolis, like crowded areas and uneven lighting. The following sophisticated advice will assist you in navigating these complexities:

1. Make use of natural lines and leading lines: roads, buildings, bridges, and other unique architectural elements are frequently seen in urban settings and can function as leading lines. To create a sense of movement and direction, place your subjects along these lines, which will pull the viewer's eye into the frame.

2. Try Different Angles: Don't be scared to photograph from high or low angles. While a low angle might highlight the subject against tall skyscrapers, a lofty perspective can offer a distinctive vision of the city. Make use of your GoPro's adaptability to record these different viewpoints, which will add to the shots' dynamic quality.

3. Take Pictures at Various Times of Day: From sunrise to sunset, the urban landscape undergoes a significant change. While the golden hour brings warmth and drama, the early mornings offer gentler light and fewer people. On the other hand, different vitality and neon lights are present in the evening. Try these times to see what mood works best for your subject.

4. Use Motion Blur: Fast-moving subjects, such as runners, skateboarders, and cyclists, are frequently featured in urban action. Think of introducing motion blur with a slower shutter speed to highlight their speed. By capturing the spirit of movement, this approach allows the viewer to experience the excitement of the action.

5. Capture Unplanned Moments: Unplanned moments can yield the best action images in urban environments. Prepare to shoot on the spur of the moment; sometimes the most memorable shots are the ones that capture the unexpected. Remain vigilant and prepare your camera to capture ephemeral events as they happen.

Natural Settings

Appreciating the Magnificent Outdoors

Photographing motion in natural environments, such as mountains, beaches, or forests, presents both the beauty and difficulties of nature, like shifting light and unpredictability in the weather. Here's how to deal with these settings:

1. Recognize Natural Light: Natural light is subject to quick changes. For example, beautiful photographs with rich colors and gentle shadows can be captured during the golden hour immediately following sunrise or before sunset. To add atmosphere to your photos, pay attention to how the light changes and take advantage of it.

2. Select the Correct Settings: To freeze motion in strong daylight, especially when photographing moving subjects like sports or wildlife, use a high shutter speed. On the other hand, change your ISO settings in low-light conditions while keeping in mind that your photos may contain noise. Although the GoPro Hero 13 does well in low light, it is important to understand how to adjust its settings.

3. Make Use of Natural Frames: To improve your composition, seek out natural framing elements like trees, rock formations, or waterfalls. These frames highlight the subject while giving the picture depth, context, and a sense of location.

4. Stay Dry and Protected: Make sure your GoPro is waterproof and think about utilizing protective housing when shooting in rainy circumstances. This not only protects your equipment but also creates opportunities for breathtaking action photos near the water or in the rain, where splashes and reflections can produce lovely effects.

5. Be Observant and Patient: Nature photography frequently calls for patience. Spend some time taking in your surroundings and waiting for the ideal opportunity to act spontaneously. Capturing these authentic moments, such as a hiker reaching the mountain or a bird taking flight, can produce striking photographs.

Preserving the Excitement

In order to portray the passion and excitement of action sports like surfing, snowboarding, or mountain biking, one needs to have quick reflexes and a sharp eye. The following sophisticated advice is tailored to these high-stress situations:

1. Know Your Subject: It's important to comprehend the subtleties of the sport you're photographing. Discover the typical motions, gimmicks, and scenes that characterize the action. This information will help you determine when and where to aim for best results.

2. Find the Correct Position: In action sports photography, positioning is crucial. Plan your route in advance and identify areas with the best views. This might be close to a skate park, at a surf break, or along a ski slope. Getting the right angle can help capture action intensity.

3. Select Continuous Shooting Mode: For action-packed scenes, the GoPro Hero 13 has burst shooting modes that are perfect. By using this tool, you can take numerous frames per second and choose the greatest moment from a collection of pictures. In sports photography, where time is crucial, this is really helpful.

4. Try Slow Motion: The GoPro Hero 13 is a fantastic camera for creating excellent slow-motion videos. Try using this tool to highlight action sports' dynamism by producing dramatic scenes that highlight the subtleties of movement.

5. Include Background Elements: Take into account the background when photographing action sports. Contextualizing your action pictures with elements like breaking waves or towering mountains might improve the narrative you're presenting. Make sure the background enhances your subject rather than detracts from it.

Adjusting to various weather situations

The weather has a big influence on the shooting process and the final product of your photos, and it can be unpredictable. The following advice may help you adjust your photos to different weather conditions:

1. Sunny Days: To improve colors and lessen glare on bright days, apply polarizing filters. This will add color to your action photographs by saturating your images and making the skies jump.

2. Overcast Days: Soft, diffused light produced by a cloudy sky is perfect for lessening harsh shadows. This eliminates the influence of intense sunlight, making it ideal for capturing details in action images. Make the most of this lighting by emphasizing expressions and textures.

3. Rainy Conditions: Your photos can gain drama and emotion from the rain. Accept the rain and think about using a quick shutter speed to capture moving raindrops. Make sure your camera has waterproof housing, and don't be afraid to capture the beauty of the damp setting.

4. Snowy Landscapes: Snow offers special chances as well as difficulties. To make sure details are preserved, try adjusting your exposure in manual mode because the white landscape can confuse exposure settings. Because the snowflakes lend a sense of wonder to the activity, photographing during a snowfall can provide wonderful photographs.

5. Windy Conditions: The movement of the subject and the steadiness of your photographs can both be impacted by wind. To reduce shake, use a tripod or steady your GoPro. To capture the sense of motion without sacrificing clarity, carefully position oneself when taking pictures of things in windy conditions.

Examples from the Real World:

Success Stories

Let's look at a few real-world instances to demonstrate these pointers and show how comprehension of the action environment may produce amazing outcomes.

Example 1: Forest Mountain Biking

A mountain cyclist riding through a deep forest on a tight, meandering track is photographed. They employed a low-angle image to highlight the rider against the tall trees, and they exploited the path's natural lines to draw the viewer's attention to the subject. They created a mystical interplay of light and shadow by arranging their shot to take place just as a sunbeam was penetrating the foliage, giving the movement more dimension.

Example 2: Sunset Surfing

At sunset, another photographer visits a well-known surfing location. In order to record surfers riding the waves against the vivid hues of the fading sun, they put their GoPro in continuous filming mode and positioned themselves. In order to emphasize the surfers' strength and grace as they slashed through the water, they used a slower shutter speed to produce motion blur.

Chapter 8

Gear and Accessories for Extreme Action Photography

The correct equipment and accessories can make all the difference when it comes to intense action photography. Although your GoPro Hero 13 is a strong tool by itself, when combined with the appropriate add-ons, it can assist you in taking beautiful, high-quality pictures in a range of difficult situations. This chapter offers a summary of the key GoPro accessories that daring photographers should think about, as well as professional suggestions for extra gear suited to particular action situations.

Important GoPro add-ons for adventurous photographers

1. Mounts

In order to secure your GoPro and enable steady and imaginative shots, mounts are necessary. They allow you to record action from unusual angles that would otherwise be challenging or impossible. The following are a few essential mounts for extreme action photography:

• **Chest Mount Harness:** This mount is ideal for shooting hands-free, whether kayaking, skiing, or mountain biking. You can take captivating point-of-view pictures that provide viewers with an exciting experience by holding the camera against your chest.

• **Helmet Mount:** Perfect for fans of action sports, this mount fastens straight to your helmet and provides a first-person view of your travels. This mount records every turn, whether you're riding a bike across tough terrain or snowboarding down a mountain.

- **Suction Cup attachment:** Suitable for recording action from vehicles, boats, or even drones, this adaptable attachment sticks to smooth surfaces. Place your GoPro on the edge of a kayak or the roof of a car to produce dynamic video that highlights excitement and speed.

- **Tripod Mount:** Although it's not usually connected to action photography, a tripod mount can help your GoPro stay steady when taking unusual time-lapse pictures or in low light. A tripod can offer the stability required for some photographs, particularly in situations when the ground is uneven, yet many action photographers fail to see its advantages.

2. Filters

Filters can improve the quality of your video by regulating color and light. The following filters are necessary for various shooting situations:

- **Polarizing Filter:** This filter minimizes reflections and glare, which makes it perfect for taking pictures near water or in strong light. It improves color saturation, making the vegetation more vivid and the sky bluer. Outdoor activities like hiking and fishing are especially beneficial when using a polarizing filter.

By lowering the quantity of light that enters the lens, an ND (neutral density) filter enables longer exposure periods without overexposing your image. This helps create that cinematic motion blur, which is particularly useful while filming. An ND filter can help you keep your shots looking professional when you're taking pictures of fast-moving action in direct sunshine.

• **Red Filter:** A red filter is used in underwater photography to make up for color loss caused by light leaking through water. By restoring the natural colors of underwater settings, this filter brings out the best in landscapes and aquatic life. Having a red filter on your GoPro is essential if you're diving or snorkeling.

3. Outside Stabilizers

Stabilizers are essential for producing fluid video, particularly in high-action situations where camera wobble is unavoidable. Take into account these choices for more stability:

- **Gimbal Stabilizer:** A gimbal is a sophisticated stabilizing tool that maintains your GoPro level by preventing any tremor or movement. This is especially helpful while recording while cycling, jogging, or doing other fast-paced activities. The end product is a film of expert quality that looks fluid and dramatic.

- **Handheld Stabilizer:** These stabilizers offer a balanced grip that lessens shaking when moving, making them ideal for people who prefer a more physical approach. While keeping your footage steady, these stabilizers let you experiment with your shots.

Professional Suggestions for Particular Action Situations

1. Photographing underwater

Having the appropriate equipment is crucial if you intend to go deep for some underwater action photography.

- **Underwater Housing:** A sturdy underwater housing will shield your GoPro from water harm. To guarantee safety during deep dives, look for housing that is rated for at least 40 meters (131 feet). In order to facilitate movement, some housings even have built-in handles.

• **Floating Hand Grip:** This feature helps keep your GoPro from sinking in the event that you drop it while shooting in water. Additionally, this accessory gives you more control when shooting underwater situations, so you can record every moment without worrying about misplacing your camera.

• **Wide-Angle Lens:** To capture more of the colorful underwater environment, think about utilizing a wide-angle lens adapter for underwater photography. By increasing your field of view, this lens enables you to capture more landscapes and marine life in your photographs.

2. Sports Action

Certain additions can improve your shooting experience for those exhilarating activities that call for lightning-fast reflexes and exceptional precision.

• **Pole Mounts:** By extending your reach, a pole mount enables you to record action from unusual perspectives. From a distance, you can produce breathtaking photos that showcase the action, whether you're snowboarding or surfing.

• **Mounts for skis or snowboards:** These specialist mounts firmly fasten your GoPro to your gear so you can record first-person footage of your rides. These mounts make it simple to record your runs without holding the camera, giving you more hands to use for action.

• **Remote Control:** By enabling you to start and stop filming remotely, a remote control frees you up to concentrate on the action rather than fumbling with your camera. This is useful when you don't have time to get to your camera, like on the water or doing extreme sports.

3. Photographing Travel

Having adaptable equipment is crucial while documenting your vacation experiences.

• **Travel Case:** To keep your GoPro and accessories safe and organized while traveling, get a suitable travel case. Seek out cases with movable sections so you can customize the area for your particular equipment.

• **Portable Charger:** A portable charger can keep your GoPro charged during those extended shooting days. To charge your GoPro and other gadgets at the same time, think about getting a power bank with several USB connections.

• **Smartphone App:** You can examine your photos, edit video straight from your phone, and remotely control your camera using the GoPro app. Sharing your activities instantaneously is made possible by this function, which is quite helpful while you're on the go.

Conclusion

Becoming a GoPro Action Storyteller

Keep in mind that the possibilities are endless as you start your career as a GoPro action storyteller. You can experience the excitement of catching action-packed moments and expressing your travels with breathtaking images. Never be afraid to challenge yourself; every new method you try might open your eyes to new possibilities and let your story come to life in ways you never thought possible. Every action you take enhances your creative toolset, whether it's perfecting lighting in dynamic settings, learning how to frame the ideal photo, or experimenting with perspectives that give your story dimension.

On this path, experimentation is your biggest ally. Experiment with various mounts, settings, and unusual accessories to see what suits your style the best. Capturing everything from calm landscapes to intense action images is made possible by the GoPro's versatility. Accept the process of making mistakes as you explore the world of GoPro photography. Unexpected blunders that teach you important lessons can sometimes provide the most captivating photographs.

When it comes to improving your craft, patience is essential. It takes time to become proficient with your equipment, the settings you're shooting in, and the objects you're photographing. Great photography doesn't always happen overnight. Patience will pay off handsomely, whether you're waiting for the ideal wildlife photography moment or modifying your settings in quickly shifting light circumstances.

Above all, the secret to becoming an engaging action storyteller is to hone your own style. Show off your individuality in your photographs; what distinguishes your viewpoint from others? Maybe it's how you engage with your surroundings or how you embody the spirit of the things you enjoy doing. In a world full of images, your own voice and vision will stand out to your audience. Thus, take out your GoPro, venture beyond your comfort zone, and allow your creativity to blossom. You have the opportunity to record the adventures that lie ahead, and you never know, you might encourage others to set out on their own adventures. You will develop into an exceptional storyteller in addition to a proficient action photographer with practice, perseverance, and a dedication to discovering your unique style.

www.ingramcontent.com/pod-product-compliance
Lightning Source LLC
LaVergne TN
LVHW020020121224
798917LV00040B/1250